# What Business Owners Need to Stop Doing

Book 1 in the "Stop So You Can Get the Results You Want" Series

BY

LIZ WEBER, CMC, CSP

# Also by Liz Weber, CMC, CSP

*Something Needs to Change Around Here: The Five Stages to Leveraging Your Leadership*

*Don't Let 'Em Treat You Like a Girl: A Woman's Guide to Leadership Success*

*What Managers Need to Stop Doing*

*What Human Resources Professionals Need to Stop Doing*

*What Women in Leadership Need to Stop Doing*

*Stop So You Can Get The Results You Want*

# Special Offer

If you enjoyed Liz's insights in this book, take advantage of these special offers:

1. Take Liz's Free Leadership Assessment to determine which of The Five Stages of Focused Leadership® you are currently modeling! Just go to her website, wbsllc.com, to access the assessment!

2. Click here to download Liz's white paper featuring the three things you need to stop today! Go to www.wbsllc.com/stop-it/

# Social Media

*Visit my website: http://www.WBSLLC.com*

*Or connect with me on social media:*

# What Business Owners Need to Stop Doing

Book 1 in the "Stop So You Can Get the Results You Want" Series

by Liz Weber

Published 2019 by Aspen Hill Press

This book is licensed for your personal enjoyment and education only. While best efforts have been used, the author and publisher are not offering legal, accounting, medical, or any other professional services advice and make no representations or warranties of any kind and assume no liabilities of any kind with respect to the accuracy or completeness of the contents and specifically disclaim any implied warranties of merchantability or fitness of use for a particular purpose, nor shall they be held liable or responsible to any person or entity with respect to any loss or incidental or consequential damages caused, or alleged to have been caused, directly or indirectly, by the information or programs contained herein. Stories, characters, and entities are 'sanitized' versions of real client experiences.

The information in this book on personnel management is done in an informational manner only. All personnel actions should be reviewed carefully before implementation. Please consult with your human resources professionals, legal counsel etc before taking official action to ensure you are complying with company policies, as well as any and all state and federal employment laws.

All rights reserved. No part of this publication may be reproduced or transmitted in any form or by any means, electronic or mechanical, including photocopying, recording, or by any information storage and retrieval system, without permission in writing from the publisher. All images are free to use or share, even commercially, according to Google at the time of publication unless otherwise noted. Thank you for respecting the hard work of the author(s) and everyone else involved.

Copyright © 2019, 2015 Elizabeth J. Weber,

Weber Business Services, LLC. All Rights

Reserved.

*Authors and sources cited throughout retain the*

*copyright to their respective materials.*

*This book is dedicated to my clients. You are intelligent, kind, generous, and continually striving to be not only better business owners and leaders, but better people. I respect you and thank you for the opportunity to know you and work with you.*

*—Liz*

*"Whenever you see a successful business, someone once made a courageous decision."*

*Peter F. Drucker*

# Contents

*Introduction* _____ *1*

*{ 1 } Stop Hiding the Company's Goals* _____ *11*

*{ 2 } Stop Being So Busy You Regularly Lose Focus* *27*

*{ 3 } Stop Saying You're Going to Make Changes If You're Not Willing to See Them Through* _____ *41*

*{ 4 } Stop Allowing Your Biases to Limit Your Company's Growth* _____ *51*

*{ 5 } Stop Demanding Your Management Team Improve While Ignoring Your Own Weaknesses and Shortcomings* _____ *59*

*{ 6 } Stop Treating Ill-Equipped and Under-Qualified Family Members Better Than High-Performing Team Members* _____ *73*

*{ 7 } Stop Treating Your Employees Like Untrustworthy Children* _____ *85*

*{ 8 } Stop Rewarding Perfect Attendance* _____ *99*

*{ 9 } Stop Thinking Your Business Can't Exist Without You* _____ *111*

*{ 10 } Stop Reacting and Start Leading With Intent* _____ *119*

*Conclusion* _____ *133*

*Continue Your Leadership Journey* _____ *141*

*About Liz Weber, CMC, CSP* _____ *143*

# Introduction

*"My job as a leader is to make sure everybody in the company has great opportunities, and that they feel like they're having a meaningful impact."*

— *Larry Page, CEO, Google*

**OWNING AND LEADING** a business is tough, and not everyone can do it. As the business owner, you have the power to either make useful changes that will lead to a better future for your company, your employees, and your customers, or to keep repeating the same unproductive practices over and over while wishing for better results. The first option seems an obvious desired choice, yet most business owners flounder in the zone of the second more often than not. Why? They're not consistently doing what they need to do to create the type of businesses they want. As a result, they're floundering and so are their companies. Let's ensure that doesn't happen to you.

To ensure you get the most out of the ten different ideas I'll share in this book, let's take a few steps back to clarify why you're a business owner in the first place. Because let's be honest, we as business owners deal with more responsibility, stress, and risk than do managers without any promise of success. If our businesses fail, not only will the lives and financial security of all of our employees be impacted, but we also may lose our personal as well as business assets. So why do it? Why put ourselves in that type of situation?

Because the alternative of *not* being your own boss and having your own business is simply not an option for you. So let's ensure you continue to build the type of business you want.

**Why Did You Become a Business Owner?**

From my experience, many small to mid-sized business owners started their own businesses, or took over the family business because they wanted to:

- Be their own bosses
- Have the freedom to determine their own professional futures
- Build and create something from nothing
- Fill a need
- Be able to pursue a personal mission or passion
- Achieve greater financial wealth
- Have control over the types of people with whom they work and the type of work they do

- Create a lifestyle not available to them in prior positions
- Take over the family business
- Have control

Be clear in why you became a business owner. If it wasn't the life you chose but instead you were forced into it, business ownership may not be right for you. But if you *did* intentionally become a business owner, hold onto that initial desire and keep it in focus. It will help you minimize or negate many of the distracting, non-helpful behaviors I'll be outlining in this book.

*As a business owner, keep in mind and focused on why you're in business; it'll help you achieve what you want.*

As varied are the reasons for starting a business, so too are business owners' ambitions for themselves and their businesses. In working with my strategic and succession planning clients for over 20 years, I've worked with business owners who wanted to do one or more of the following:

- Make a lot of money
- Create something from nothing
- Dominate their industries
- Build businesses to support their children and grandchildren
- Build a business they could sell so they could retire
- Create businesses and develop the management teams to run daily operations so they wouldn't have to themselves
- Pass a legacy business on to their children
- Provide safe, well-paying jobs for as many people as possible

*Why* you became a business owner is important to keep fresh in your mind because that rationale is one of your business' missions. *What* you hoped to achieve when you started your business is one of your driving business strategies - if not the vision for your company. When you lose track of *why* you're doing *what* you're supposed to be doing, you're constantly busy, yet you don't ever truly move forward and accomplish what you intended. As a business owner, keep in mind and stay focused on *why* you're in business; it'll help you achieve *what* you want.

*Become the business owner and leader your company needs you to be.*

Business ownership is tough. Lots of studies have been done on the number of new businesses that fail, and the numbers are staggering. Different studies report different statistics, but even the most optimistic reports estimate that 30% of all businesses fail within 5-10 years. Some researchers have found that number to be closer to 70 or even 80%. No one said it was easy and you knew that going in. Yet, you still made the choice to become a business owner and its leader. With that choice comes responsibility. So, for the sake of your business's future, increase the odds of success by doing what your company needs you to do to survive and thrive. Stop doing several things that are holding you, your employees, and your company back from achieving everything you want and more. Become the business owner and leader your company needs you to be.

# { 1 } Stop Hiding the Company's Goals

*"To succeed in business it is necessary to make others see things as you see them."*

*— John H. Patterson, Founder of NCR Corporation*

**WHY: UNLIKE THE** movie *City Slickers* in which Billy Crystal's character learns that "The One Thing" in life that will make a person happy is different for everyone; in business, we need to make it explicitly clear to all of our employees what we're trying to achieve as an organization --

together. If we don't, we're forcing our employees to guess at what we want them to be doing and working towards. When our employees guess at what they think we want them to be doing, they each create their own version of the desired outcome, and subsequently, they each head off in a slightly different direction. We've now created a situation where our employees are working towards varied outcomes. They're not leveraging each other's work, and they're wasting precious time and resources, although they're each trying hard to do what they believe is expected.

Several years ago, I was asked by Taylor, the owner of a small professional services firm to facilitate his company's strategic plan update session. They'd created their company's strategic plan themselves, but Taylor thought it would be useful to have a consultant facilitate their update process. His company's performance had stalled during the previous year, the management team seemed to be battling each other more than working together, and the entire company's morale was lower than it had been in years. Taylor was sure his young management team simply needed someone from the outside to help develop their skills in understanding and working a company's strategic plan.

Soon after I started their update session, I understood why they'd stalled. No one knew the plan! When I started the session, I simply asked the entire team, "To get an idea of what you're working towards as a company, what is your company's vision?" I was met with the proverbial deer-caught-in-the-headlights look from the entire team (except the two managers who were rifling through their files trying to find a copy of the vision). It was obvious the company's vision wasn't something the leadership team used as a focusing tool for business decisions and strategies, as no manager knew it. As his team of managers scrambled to find a copy of the vision, Taylor grunted and looked at his team in frustration. So I asked him to share his company's vision. Taylor suddenly looked a bit nervous and rather clumsily clarified that he'd revised the vision a few months ago to make it more attainable. However, because it hadn't changed dramatically he hadn't formally released it to the management team; he had wanted to wait for this planning session to formally review it with them and release it. Taylor had been waiting for a once-a-year event in order to share critical company information with his senior team. I was stunned. The managers were rightly angry.

As we continued, I was amazed the company's performance hadn't stalled more than it had. When I asked the managers to provide updates on the corporate goals they'd been working on over the prior year, I again was presented with nervous looks and hesitation. After a few uncomfortable seconds, Taylor stated, "We really don't have one set of goals this team has monitored together. The goals we created last year changed, and I've found it's been more productive for me to simply work one-on-one with a manager or a few project-related managers to tell them what I need, instead of having to pull my entire senior team in to a meeting to discuss goals. Those meetings invariably take longer and aren't as productive as the smaller one-on-ones."

In the spirit of open-mindedness, I asked again for the managers to share what company goals they'd each been working on with Taylor so I could hear directly from them what action had been taking place within the company and management team. I'd already heard Taylor's version of reality. As the various managers relayed their goals and the work they'd done, invariably their colleagues who were not involved with a particular goal, started saying things such as:

*So that's what you've been working on! I couldn't figure out why you've been so focused on the Jenson Data release status. Huh, that's really cool.*

*I've never heard of that before.*

*Is that what we used to call the Liberty Project?*

*If you and Dan are now handling that, am I supposed to have Janita and Travis stop or are they going to be working with you and Dan at some point too?*

*When was that decided?*

*Why are you working on that? My team's been gathering data on that for the past three months?*

*Can I ask why I wasn't included in this project?*

As the conversation and questions continued, Taylor was physically becoming agitated and embarrassed. It was obvious the entire senior management team had questions of him, each other, and the work they were supposed to be doing. In an attempt to increase his individual senior manager's productivity, he'd succeeded in increasing confusion, frustration, duplicated efforts, and hard feelings among his senior management team and within their respective departments.

To ensure I had a complete picture, I asked one final question, "Would it be fair for me to assume you have not provided any company updates to your employees on any of these goals?" Taylor and his managers sheepishly replied, "That'd be an accurate assumption."

By not managing his senior team meetings well, by not regularly reviewing and updating the company and team goals with his senior managers, by not doing his job of consistently ensuring his senior team was working from the same master plan of goals, and by not providing regular company updates on the goals, he'd created problems for his managers, the employees, and his company. They were working harder than they needed to. They weren't leveraging one another's work, and they were duplicating efforts. By trying to save time and not sharing the goals, he'd held his company back from moving forward.

*By trying to save time by not consistently sharing the company goals, you hold your company back.*

**Here's what I suggest you do instead:** Let your employees know specifically what it is you want your company to achieve and how they fit in. Let them know how each department or position is expected to help move your company closer to its vision. Share your goals and expectations, but then make sure everyone understands them and can therefore help them become reality.

To do a quick self-check on how well you've been communicating your company's vision and goals, take this simple challenge: Walk around and ask five to ten random employees, "What is the number one thing this organization is trying to achieve?" If you get roughly the same answer from each of the employees, you've done an excellent—and I mean excellent—job of communicating your vision and creating focus for your employees. If your question is answered with confused looks, "I don't knows", or five to ten different answers, you've not yet done a few things employees need from you to help them do their jobs well: Provided direction, focus, a target (i.e., a Vision), or goals.

If you've got confusion instead of clarity, set aside some dedicated time and clarify your vision and goals with your managers and employees. Tell them your vision if you're comfortable doing so. If your vision is a financial target you'd rather not make known to your managers or employees, that's fine. Then you at least need to share with them a few of your company's strategic goals for the year so they can understand there is a reason for many of the activities they're asked to support.

Meet with your managers at least quarterly, if not monthly, to review—as a team—the status of your company's vision and/or strategic goals. Give them an opportunity to brainstorm, debate, and share ideas to leverage one another's efforts to help you move your company forward.

Also, each quarter, provide basic, quick updates to all employees on the company's progress towards or away from the goals and/or vision. Let them know when you're making progress; let them know when you've had set backs. Minimize their surprises and need to guess as to what's happening. Your employees are going to be more engaged and interested in what the company is doing if they're able to track its progress (and their supporting efforts) towards or away from the goals and vision.

*"Sharing information with employees makes them feel invested."*

*— Glen Mazzara, television writer and producer*

# { 2 } Stop Being So Busy You Regularly Lose Focus

*"So often people are working hard at the wrong thing.*

*Working on the right thing is probably more important than working hard."*

— *Caterina Fake, co-founder of Flicker*

**WHY: WHEN YOU** appear uncertain, scattered, and unfocused, it's not only difficult for you to stay focused and productive; it's difficult for anyone who works with you to stay focused and productive as well. You're not only sending confusing messages, you're wasting energy—yours and theirs. You're demonstrating "buckshot" leadership versus "laser" leadership. When you shoot buckshot from a shotgun, the cartridge explodes upon firing. It spreads buckshot pellets across a wide area with the anticipation that one or more pellets will hit the target, while the rest of the pellets are wasted or hit unintended targets. A laser, on the other hand, sends a beam of light at its target. A laser is focused and sends its light (i.e. its energy) at one thing and one thing only.

If you think this lack-of-focus behavior doesn't relate to you, great. But go ahead and review these questions to ensure you would answer "NO" to every one of them:

*Are you exhausted at the end of every workday?*

*Do you lay in bed at night worrying about how you're going to get everything done?*

*Are you regularly trying to identify new ways to bring in more sales, increase business, or in some other way "get ahead"?*

If you answered "No" to every one of these questions, that's great. Good for you. However, if you're like most business owners, you probably answered "Yes" to at least one of them.

If you did, join the club. You're like most hard-working business owners. Notice, I said you're like most 'hard-working' business owners. I didn't say you're like most 'successful' business owners. There's a big difference and the difference lies in how the hard-working work versus how the successful work.

Several years ago, I worked with Lena, a new business owner, in Guatemala. Lena had bought the business nine months prior and had been excited about its possibilities. However, now after nine long months, Lena was overwhelmed and struggling with exhaustion and frustration. After years of neglect and lackluster management, her production facility had so many areas that needed attention; it seemed as if she'd never turn it into the company she'd dreamed it could be.

When I arrived for our first work session, Lena was on the phone, had two other calls on hold, and she was surrounded by piles of papers. When she completed her three immediate phone calls, she muted her phone so we wouldn't be interrupted again. We then started to review her unending "To Do" list. As Lena explained the items on her list, many of the items she considered "important" weren't. They simply needed to be addressed at some point in time, but they weren't important at that moment. As Lena shared more of what she was working on and what she knew she needed to address, it became clear why Lena was spinning out of control: Lena was attempting to do "everything" immediately, and she was doing too many tactical things herself. Because of this, she was losing sight of what she needed to focus on as the business owner, and it was why she was burning out. Lena was expending so much of her energy doing things that were less important but were "quicker fixes," that when she faced something truly important, she was too tired to tackle it. So the truly important and business-changing strategies weren't getting done. She'd put them off until she had more time, energy, and money to deal with them. Lena was using the buckshot approach and not the laser approach.

Lena was working hard trying to accomplish many small things, just to get *something* done. She was working on projects that were important to her, but they weren't going to help her business move in the direction she wanted it to move quickly. Because of this, she was making small improvements here and there, but she wasn't addressing the serious problems that had domino-like ramifications if they weren't addressed quickly and properly.

When we re-worked her "To Do" list, we focused on addressing the most serious and the most far-reaching issues first. As we worked through this exercise and identified her critical path, we were able to eliminate many items from her original list. They became non-issues or were resolved indirectly once the overarching problems were addressed.

Lena's "To Do" list got shorter. It focused on leveraging many items on her list for greater impact. Most helpful to her, it also then highlighted the actions that only she, as the business owner, needed to focus on and address. Things that would help her company, her employees, and her customers.

*There's a big difference in working hard and in working smartly.*

**Here's what I suggest you do instead:** Work on what is truly important and forget or eliminate the rest. It's a leadership technique every one of us in business has heard many times before, yet many fail to use. However, to stop working hard and start working more smartly, limit your focus and energies. Ask yourself every day, "What do I need to do today to help move this company forward?"

In observing my successful and my less-successful clients over the past 20+ years, my more successful clients follow this rule. The less successful don't. As a result, the less successful work very hard, doing the same things many different ways, while making incremental progress. They inch their way forward, while other business owners seemingly breeze by, achieving things the hard-working business owners have been working towards for years. How do they do that?

They stay focused on what's important. If an opportunity (i.e. a strategy, a project, a goal, a tactic, a task, an initiative or any other name you want to attach to it) doesn't clearly help move the company forward, it's dropped. Energies and hard work are not wasted on "interesting" or "potentially helpful" activities. The successful business owners' energies and hard work are reserved for strategically helpful activities.

When you've clarified for yourself what the most important things to focus on and work towards are for your organization, you need to clarify, communicate, and regularly repeat that focus to your teams as well. The truly successful business owners have instilled in their teams an understanding of how their roles and jobs are important to the organization. The team members know how they each best add value to the overall organization by keying into specific aspects of each job. The successful business owner has also pushed the responsibility to focus on working smartly instead of simply working hard to each employee. As such, their employees regularly think about the work they're doing and to confirm its value. If what they're doing isn't adding value or helping the business move forward, why are they doing it? Focus. Think. Don't just do. Stop working hard. Start working smartly with focus.

*"The bottom line is, when people are crystal clear about the most important priorities of the organization... not only are they many times*

*more productive, they discover they have the time they need to have a whole life."*

— *Stephen Covey, author, The Seven Habits of Highly Effective People*

# { 3 } Stop Saying You're Going to Make Changes If You're Not Willing to See Them Through

*"Successful people tend to have a high need for self-determination. In other words, the more leaders commit to coaching and behavioral change because they believe in the value of the process, the more likely the process is to work."*

— *Marshall Goldsmith, author, What Got You Here Won't Get You There*

**WHY: WHEN YOU** tell your management team and your employees you're going to make the long-awaited changes to the company, and then you don't, it should be no surprise that you lose credibility. You also greatly reduce their inclination to offer future suggestions for changes and improvements. From their perspective: *Why bother identifying needed improvements? You aren't going to make the changes anyway.*

After having worked with Terry and his management team for over nine months crafting a three-year strategic plan, and mapping out both a short-term emergency and long-term staffing plan, it was time to implement. It was time to start changing policies, re-aligning departments, re-aligning responsibilities, re-aligning positions, changing people in positions, and re-aligning the business' infrastructure to support the company as it moved forward toward its new vision. The company infrastructure and management practices that had allowed the company to grow to its current size were no longer capable of supporting the desired growth outlined in the new strategic plan.

The rollout was flawless; Terry's energy and that of the leadership team spread throughout the organization. In just the first six months of the new plan, short-term goals started were met with wild success and several difficult but long-overdue personnel actions were taken. It wasn't easy, but Terry acknowledged, "These changes are long overdue."

When I work with companies to change their businesses and leadership practices, I warn every client, "If you truly want change, realize it will take a minimum of 18 to 36 months of dedicated effort for any new initiative to become 'normal'. Organizational and leadership change doesn't happen quickly."

When I returned for an 18-month review, Terry and his leadership team were facing many of the same issues as other leadership teams pushing forward major changes: change is a long-term, painful process. The members of the management team had started to experience the plateaus of excitement. *This is no longer new and different. This is now a pain!*

They had each experienced the frustration at the slowness of change in others. *Why don't the employees change the way they think and behave? They still default to what's comfortable instead of what's right!*

They had had eruptions and finger-pointing moments up and down the leadership chain. *It's the senior team's fault! It's the middle managers' fault! It's the fault of those front-line supervisors!*

They had been working with the frustrations of the changes "interfering" with "real" work. *We seem to meet more than before to talk things through. It takes time away from getting the work done. We're a small organization with managers who have to be doers at times too! If we're meeting and talking all the time, there's no one to do the work!*

They had each felt the frustrations of their leadership team and their own teams "backsliding" during the change process. *We're backsliding. We're spinning our wheels!*

Each of their experiences was painful, stressful, and very real. Yet when I asked Terry and the team a few questions to gauge how dedicated and intentional they had been to the change process, their responses were telling:

Are you adjusting your leadership style to lead the teams as they currently need to be led? *Not consistently. Well, we're trying to when we focus on it.*

Are you providing clear, consistent, continuous communication up, down, and across the organization? *No. We've told the supervisors to communicate more, but they're not doing it consistently and they're not communicating very clearly.*

Are you keeping the entire organization regularly apprised on how the organization is doing in moving forward on the strategic plan? *No. We've had a lot of changes in the business over the past several months and we really haven't had time.*

Are you taking the time to train people, have "Necessary Conversations™" with employees immediately to provide feedback, and use those learning opportunities as on-the-spot training opportunities? *Some. We're getting better at that.*

Are you modeling the types of behaviors you expect of everyone? Living the Values? *For the most part. We still tend to be reactionary and over-committed more than pro-active, and strategic. We've cancelled a lot of meetings and other things lately because we're all so busy.*

So what's changed? You wanted a more focused, strategic, engaged, productive, workforce and leadership team, yet you've not changed to support the new behaviors and practices. If you want things to change...you need to...change.

*If you want things to change...you need to...change.*

**Here's what I suggest you do instead:** If you want your organization and team to change, you need to change the way you lead. And, you need to keep changing.

Change is hard. Changing the way you think, behave, work, and lead others is really hard. It takes dedicated, intentional focus. It takes dedicated, intentional restraint. It takes dedicated, intentional action. It takes dedication to change.

*"Confront your inadequacies and push your personal boundaries: It's the surest way to grow, improve, and expand the scope of your influence."*

*—John C. Maxwell, author, The 21 Indispensible Qualities of a Leader: Becoming the Person Others Will Want to Follow*

# { 4 } Stop Allowing Your Biases to Limit Your Company's Growth

*"Perceptual bias can affect nut jobs and scientists alike. If we hold too rigidly to what we think we know, we ignore or avoid evidence of anything that might change our mind."*

— *Martha Beck, bestselling author and life coach*

**WHY: IF UNCHECKED,** the business owner's biases can change the tone of casual conversations with team members, as well as completely distort leadership team brainstorming or planning sessions. A disparaging look, a grunt, a huff of frustration, or an outright, adamant "Hell no!" can quickly transform an open, energetic, idea-generating work session into a subdued conversation with limited input and overwhelming tension.

In a recent client planning session, I again witnessed a business owner's biases and his unwillingness to listen deflate a team of vice presidents. As part of the work with this client, I was also coaching Brian, the business owner, on running more productive and focused meetings. To provide him with a facilitated opportunity to practice, I asked Brian to lead one portion of a pre-planning work session, whereby we allowed each senior manager time to present a strategic initiative that would help drive the company forward.

As I observed and coached Brian through the process of gaining input from each senior team member, his personal biases towards individual team members and their ideas became more and more clear. Brian heard his team members' words, but he didn't listen to their messages. His biases kept getting in the way.

As various managers tried to share their ideas, Brian wasn't listening to their *current* messages. Instead, his mind had jumped ahead and was anticipating the direction the team members' similar messages had taken in the past—and they'd not been ones Brian had liked. Therefore, anticipating more of the same, Brian would interrupt various team members, step on their comments, and negate their ideas before a manager had finished speaking.

Needless to say, if it had been left unchecked, his biases and preferences in what was shared, discussed, or debated would have completely killed the team's energy, drive, and idea generation. Luckily with a few subtle reminders, Brian stopped interrupting. However, he'd already made his biases known, and the team's ideas for the rest of the session were less robust and more in-line with the ideas Brian had introduced early in the session. Needless to say, Brian and I worked on this after the session and I facilitated all subsequent sessions to maintain objectivity while allowing for debate.

*Don't let your biases get in the way. Listen to the ideas of others.*

**Here's what I suggest you do instead:** Realize and accept that you have biases. We all do. However, as the business owner and as the leader, it's up to you to gauge how your biases may be enhancing or hindering your team's thoughts and actions—and as a result—how they may be enhancing or hindering your company's performance. Are your biases overshadowing ideas that could propel your organization forward? Are your biases towards individual team members causing you to not listen to their concerns or ideas? Are your biases causing you to block messages that could transform the way you, your team, and your entire organization operate?

If you have a team member or members who have historically had so many bad ideas or are so disruptive that you immediately tune them out, why are they still working for you? Are your biases limiting your company's growth?

*"A leader who confines his role to his people's experience dooms himself to stagnation."*

*— Henry Kissinger, former Secretary of State*

# { 5 } Stop Demanding Your Management Team Improve While Ignoring Your Own Weaknesses and Shortcomings

*"I think leadership comes from integrity—that you do whatever you ask others to do."*

— Scott Berkun, bestselling author and speaker

**WHY: NOT EVERY** business owner is a natural manager or leader. Yet when a business owner fails to supplement or develop his or her weak management and leadership skills, while simultaneously demanding the management team improve theirs, leadership hypocrisy is apparent and morale suffers.

Many business owners are business owners because they were technically quite skilled at something or because they created something that others wanted. They are true inventors, artists, craftsmen, or talented in some other way. Because of their creative skills, the demand for the businesses' products or services enabled their companies to hire additional staff, offer additional products and services, and expand into additional facilities and markets. All of this requires management and leadership skills, which may not necessarily be among the business owners' strong skill sets.

Steve's father started a manufacturing facility in the family garage, and Steve has worked for the company for over thirty years. He started when he was a teenager. His first job was sweeping floors. He then worked in every aspect of production, steadily working his way up through the company's hierarchy, including serving as Vice President of Production, to now sitting in the President's chair. When he took over as the company's owner and president 15 years earlier, after his father died, Steve had personally and tirelessly, spearheaded the company's growth from a 90-person operation to over 150 people; from less than $10 million in annual revenues to almost $40 million. He personally oversaw every major decision, negotiation, and action that had allowed the company to grow to its current levels. However, he knew he needed stronger leadership and management skills to take the company over the $40 million dollar mark.

As he shared with me, "Liz, I can grow a company, but I don't know how to develop leadership skills. I've got good people; they just have weak management and leadership skills. Myself included. I've been winging it so far, but I know I've hit my limits."

As we moved forward, Steve and his management team worked on creating clear, focused and workable strategic and workforce plans. The team focused intently on modeling and honing behaviors and techniques practiced during leadership training and projects. They each identified specific ways they needed to change behaviors, both individually and as a team, in order to ensure the company could continue to grow and their employees could continue to develop. The management team started identifying opportunities to apply techniques learned in training.

They started letting go of old habits, and they delegated and shared information. The employees started to notice a difference. The employees were given more opportunities to provide input, but they were also being held accountable to contribute and not just show up. Things were different.

However, as the changes started to occur with the frontline, mid-level, and senior staff, the pressure built on Steve to also change. The realignment of responsibilities with his senior staff was positioning them to take over more of the responsibilities Steve had controlled for over 20 years. Yet he'd resist relinquishing control of key areas that drove production and global customer relations—the two key areas that drove their business. When asked why he still controlled these two areas of the business, his standard reply was, "I can't risk this now. If I'm not intimately involved, one mistake could cost us millions." Without Steve changing his mindset and trusting others to learn to do the work, all the changes made by the rest of the staff and the management team meant nothing.

Needless to say, some of the transformative strategic changes stalled because of the roadblock Steve created by not relinquishing control and getting out of his team's way. His managers wanted to take on additional responsibilities to implement more changes and new techniques, but without Steve letting go of work he - as the company's president - didn't need to do, the managers were stuck.

I bumped into Steve in an airport one year later. Because it'd been awhile since I'd worked with him and his team, I asked, "How are things going?" He looked embarrassed, hesitated, and then said:

*"Well to be honest, not good. John took a job as VP of Production for another company. We lost one of our largest customers, the economy is still hurting us, employees are really nervous about our future, and I'm travelling a lot these days. We've lost money this past year. We still haven't taken on the full reorganization we planned—and we should have. I hope it's not too*

*late. I'm not making excuses, but sometimes I feel as if I'm damned if I make a change but I'm also damned if I don't. I know the management team is frustrated with me, but I just couldn't risk someone screwing up production when we had the orders coming in. I guess I held on too tightly to what I knew. I hope it's not too late."*

In an attempt to find a light in this situation, I continued, "Steve just because you didn't implement the big initiatives and you're still doing the work you and your team said you needed to delegate three years ago, it doesn't mean all is lost. You and the team had a great deal of momentum going in making more subtle improvements.

Are you and the management team reviewing your strategic plan regularly? *No*

Are you still meeting with the management team regularly to keep them informed of company issues and to allow them to communicate across departments to develop better working relationships? *No*

Are you still focusing on training to develop your employees and management team to build skills and talent deep and wide within your organization? *No. I stopped that because we were losing money.*

I stopped asking questions. The man obviously was anxious about his company, frustrated with the lack of progress, and embarrassed by his failure to commit to the strategic and managerial changes. "Steve, you're human. But you are the president of the company and you know, with that sexy title comes incredible responsibility for making decisions. What strategies and management changes occur—or do not occur—are your choice. It's all in committing to changing yourself first so you can help your team and company change."

Steve looked at me and said, "Let's do this." And he did.

*Commit to changing yourself first so you can help your team and company change.*

**Here's what I suggest you do instead:** If you want your management team, employees and others to improve and change, you need to lead by example.

If you know you have management and leadership weaknesses, admit them. No one is perfect and your team will respect you more for admitting your weaknesses they have already seen and experienced.

Then, do the hard part: Be an example for your team of how to pick one skill to focus on, learn, hone, and do. Share with your team what you are trying to improve. Let them know it will be a process and a journey for you to develop the skill(s). You'll be successful at times; unsuccessful at others. But you'll be showing them how to be open to learn, improve, and grow. Show them how it's done. Commit to making a change, then make it.

Change is hard. It's risky. There are unknowns. There are no guarantees, but there are also rewards. If you, as the business owner, can regularly identify and improve one skill after another, you increase the potential to create an organization, were everyone—the owner included—is continually learning, growing, and improving. Now, wouldn't that be a cool place to work?

*"I have always felt that my role is to practice what I preach and make sure I lead by example. At the same time, I have to show that I am human too… It's not always about being a perfectionist. Sometimes you have to demonstrate a sense of realism."*

*— James Caan, founder, Alexander Mann, Humana International, and others*

# { 6 } Stop Treating Ill-Equipped and Under-Qualified Family Members Better Than High-Performing Team Members

*"The presumption that because you share a surname with someone who is good at their job, you'll be good at it too, is patently nonsense."*

—Dea Birkett, journalist, *"Never Too Old For Detention,"* The Guardian, July 27, 2000

**WHY: DELICATE FAMILY** relationships are an inevitable aspect of family businesses, and everyone understands that family ties are strong. However, when you promote family members over non-family members who are equally or more qualified, don't be surprised when resentment among non-family members starts to build. If the family/non-family member relationships are not managed well, non-family members may feel as if they have to "carry" the family members and "cover" for them.

At times, non-family member employees may worry about being blamed for allowing a family member to fail. In family businesses, it's not uncommon for non-family members to feel under-appreciated and used as a means for family member gain. Needless to say, family and non-family member relationships in family-owned businesses need to be managed well and intentionally.

Over a 20-year timeframe, Katherine had built her professional services firm to a 50-employee operation. In her market, her company was a market leader and had established a solid reputation for doing quality work. As the business owner, she recognized her next challenge was to develop her management team to step up and take on greater responsibilities to enable her to transition out of day-to-day operations over the next three years. A key player in the management team's development was her 25-year-old son, Ryan. It was

Katherine's hope that he would be able to take over the business one day. The problem from a leadership perspective was: Ryan wasn't respected as a manager or leader.

In his four years with the company, Ryan had been promoted from field technician, to Tech Team Supervisor, to Manager of Field Operations. He was a good worker and got along well with his fellow employees when he was a field technician. However, as Tech Team Supervisor and now Manager of Field Operations, he alienated employees. He got projects done. He met budgets. He ensured projects closed with a profit. However, he did it with a short temper, outbursts of anger and cussing rants when projects ran into problems, and a very low tolerance for any employee who didn't work as hard or as fast as he thought they should. Ryan quickly earned the nickname, "The Terminator" because he'd fire an employee quicker than the human resources office could staff new people.

As part of her company's leadership development process, Katherine decided to create a Vice President position to groom and serve as her designated second-in-command. The Vice President's role would oversee Field Operations, as well as Administration and IT. Colleen, an 18-year veteran with the company was Manager of Administration, and Danny, an experienced IT manager and six-year company employee, served as Manager of IT.

Both had served as key advisors and solid managers to Katherine over the years. Both had served as her informal second-in-command individually as well as a team during her absences over the years. However, when Katherine named Ryan Vice President during a leadership team meeting, Colleen and Danny sat in stunned silence. Later Danny shared, "I guess experience and loyalty don't count for anything around here. If you're not family, you don't matter."

Danny resigned one week later.

**Here's what I suggest you do instead:** If you bring family members into the company with the intention they take over the ownership and/or leadership of the company in the future, let your employees know that. It's OK to make that plan clear. Your non-family member employees already know it's a possibility that that's your intention. However, it may not be, and that means there are still leadership roles open to non-family members. If the non-family members know what the plan is, it enables them to plan. They can then choose to stay—knowing they probably won't ascend to the top spots—or they can choose to leave and seek employment with a firm with greater senior leadership opportunities.

Does Katherine have the right to name her son to the Vice President position? Absolutely. Does she have an obligation to communicate more honestly with her team about her goals for her son? Yes. Could communicating more effectively have mitigated the hurt and frustration Colleen and Danny felt? Probably so. It certainly would have been more transparent to her non-family member, loyal employees.

Remember: You have an obligation to family and non-family members in ensuring the organization survives and thrives into the future. As you identify what positions and skill sets your organization will need 2, 3, 4 + years into the future, create a clear staffing plan and organizational hierarchy that everyone understands. If family members believe they should move into select positions of responsibility, work with them to help them understand why someone else is more qualified. Not everyone will be happy with the structure of the organization all the time, but communication can help smooth over awkward situations, while providing time for family and non-family members alike to develop the needed skills to support, manage, and lead the organization in the future.

Stew Leonard, founder and owner of a very successful food retailer in Connecticut has had several of his children work in his stores over the years. At one point, his son was working in the produce department, but wasn't living up to his manager's expectations. The manager brought the problem to Stewart, and Stewart fired his son. Simple as that. Not all family members need to be fired, but they don't all deserve to be promoted either. Do what's best for the organization.

If some of your key employees are unhappy, it may be an unmistakable indication that there are problems facing your organization, some more difficult than others. These are, more often than not, usually serious issues that have been lurking around for some time. Without beating around the bush, too often their unhappiness is a result of your failure to address known issues such as favoring family members instead of skill. Your job as the leader is to determine what is causing your employees' discontent, obvious or not, and address it so they don't disappear and, ultimately, leave you unhappy.

*"The first rule is that family members do not work in the business unless they are at least as able as any nonfamily employee, and work at least as hard."*

*— Peter Drucker, management consultant, educator, and author*

# { 7 } Stop Treating Your Employees Like Untrustworthy Children

> *"At Semco, we treat them like adults. We trust them. We get out of their way and let them do their jobs."*
>
> — *Ricardo Semler, CEO, Semco*

**WHY: IF YOU** treat your employees like untrustworthy children, they'll act like untrustworthy children. If you micromanage them, they'll soon come to expect to be micromanaged. They won't take initiative, solve problems, make decisions, or think for themselves because you've trained them not to do so. Even the most well-intentioned, driven employees will get frustrated and become resentful when they are not given the freedom to take action, solve problems, and yes, even make mistakes and learn from them. Micromanaging will stifle well-intentioned adult behavior but will ignite distrustful childish behavior.

Complacency and micromanagement seem to be two diametrically opposed ideas. Yet complacency leads to micromanagement. And micromanagement causes employee complacency. Complacency and micromanagement feed off of one another, and yet they are mortal enemies.

So why do so many well-meaning leaders create these battles between themselves and their teams? From my experience, it's because that's how they were taught to manage. They were taught to believe that in order to manage others, you need to know your team members' jobs and to be able to do their jobs as well or better than they can. Otherwise, how can you possibly manage them? These well-meaning managers have also been taught that if your team members aren't getting the work done sufficiently, you better jump in and do the work yourself. Every one of those ideas is great on the surface.

However, what are their long-term impacts on individual and team productivity and morale, individual and team problem-solving skills, and innovation? Negative, negative, negative.

There are numerous issues to address with all of the whys and hows of micromanaging leaders, but in its most basic form, micromanaging leaders micromanage because they don't trust the judgment or work of their team members. The micromanaging leader may know this subconsciously, but the leader doesn't make the connection that that lack of trust is actually trying to serve as a huge red light indicating a staff change, employee training, or some other personnel action is needed. Simply jumping in and taking over for employees you don't trust to do the work isn't an acceptable management action. Addressing that lack of trust is. Why don't you trust your employees' judgment or abilities? What would they need to demonstrate to gain your trust? What would they need to do—specifically—over the next three, six, or nine months to start to earn your trust? Be specific in outlining what each team member would need to do to earn your trust.

During a leadership training session in which we were discussing using time productively, Kara, the Human Resources Manager, said to Lydia, the owner of the company, "I know it's been like this for years and I'm new to the company, but I don't think it's productive to have to submit all ads for a job to you for approval or to interrupt you Lydia, to get copy paper for the printer."

The other managers around the table looked stunned that Kara had made this statement. Lydia looked rather irritated but replied, "I know it may not make sense to you Kara, but it's the only way I know how to keep control of the budget and to keep track of supplies."

I didn't know what either of them were talking about, so I asked for an explanation. Lydia shared:

*"I review all ads for jobs Kara wants to place in paid advertising media to see if we can*

*cut them down a bit to save on the cost. The more words you use in the ads, the more it costs you know. And as far as the office supplies, we've had a problem in the past with employees using company supplies wastefully and also stealing some for personal use. So I keep all supplies in the trunk of my car. If someone wants something, they simply come and request it."*

I was so stunned I didn't know what to say. Lydia's drastic actions were so controlling, so limiting, I couldn't understand why more of the managers hadn't piped in. Luckily we were at the end of the session and I asked Lydia to stay to talk.

As Lydia and I talked more about the challenges with the business, staff and her actions, it became clear Lydia had had a former employee steal and betray her trust. However, as a result, Lydia was now micromanaging the remaining and new managers so intensively she was stifling their ability to do their jobs. I suggested she simply clarify for Kara what her advertising budget was and then hold Kara to it. There should be no need for Lydia to review every expense to try to reduce it.

Managers are supposed to operate within budgets. Lydia's job is to track the overall budget numbers, not the individual expenses. As for the supplies locked in her car's trunk, that was just...

odd. It was also a highly unproductive use of hers and everyone else's time. The cost of a ream of paper quadrupled every time someone needed paper because the employee would have to contact Lydia. Lydia would have to interrupt her work, physically walk to her car, retrieve the paper, and give it to the employee. The process, which should take no more than three minutes, typically took over 15 and involved two people—one being the owner of the company!

This behavior was teaching employees: If you want a 15-minute break, go ask Lydia for some office supplies and then wait for her to get them. Once Lydia and I discussed this a bit more, she agreed to move the supplies back into the supply closet, create an inventory tracking sheet, and simply monitor the supplies. If they seemed to be moving too quickly, she needed to call a meeting and talk to staff about it. Otherwise, it was costing her company money micromanaging supplies.

**Here's what I suggest you do instead:** Trust that you hired adults. Trust that your people can perform basic skills and that with proper training; they can learn the jobs they were hired to do. Allow your people to make mistakes so that they can learn. You are there to support them in their own learning processes, NOT to babysit them or try to control their every action.

As Jack Welch describes it, "Bureaucracy strangles. Informality liberates."

If you don't know what you would specifically need each team member to do to allow you to slowly trust their abilities, sit back and clarify that for yourself—and then for them. By micromanaging and not trusting them, you're encouraging their complacency. Why should they bother to do more, try harder, or solve their own problems? You'll control their actions.

So if you're tired of checking your employees' work and doing everything for your team members, stop. If you're frustrated because of your team's complacency, do something about it. Face the truth about your leadership style.

Learn to lead and manage your company and team they way they need to be led. Leverage the skills of others to move the organization forward. Don't create battles between yourself and your team members. Don't create complacency. Create clarity and accountability.

Successful leaders understand the importance of holding people accountable. Successful leaders balance accountability with collaboration and communication. Successful leaders hold their teams accountable and still let their staffs know they're appreciated.

As you reflect on your interactions with your team, ask yourself, "Am I holding my team hostage or am I holding them accountable?"

*"He who does not trust enough, will not be trusted."*

*— Lao Tzu, founder of the Taoist movement*

# { 8 } Stop Rewarding Perfect Attendance

*"It wasn't the number of hours I worked or how bloodshot my eyes were that defined the difference. It was something internal."*

—Chip Conley, founder, Joie de Vivre Hospitality

**WHY: FIRST, I'LL** share just a few of the most obvious reasons (we've all experienced in the workplace) as to why it's not a smart management move to reward perfect attendance:

**Employees with perfect attendance often:**

*1 - Come to work when they're sick—OR—when they're contagious.*

I don't think I'm alone on this one, but: I DON'T WANT TO GET SICK! Stay home when you're sick and get better there. Don't come to work and spread your germs here. If you're coming into work because you have no available sick leave or you don't want to stay home by yourself, I feel bad for you. However, you're an adult and you need to make the right choice and do what's right for your colleagues. Stay home.

*2 - Don't want to disappoint others.*

Over the years, I've heard too many managers in client organizations say they come to work when they're sick for fear they'll be viewed negatively by their bosses if they don't come into work. So the managers come to work, spread their germs, try to focus, and perform far from optimally. They're doing all of these things while their colleagues try to stay away from them so they don't get sick (see example #1 above). The sick manager is simply spreading germs and causing the team to perform unproductively as they try to avoid getting sick themselves.

*3 - Believe they're irreplaceable.*

People achieving perfect attendance often believe no one else can do their jobs. Again, I will be the bearer of bad news: Everyone is replaceable! As a business owner, you need to realize that if no one else can do an employee's job, that employee has too much control over your business, a department, or a team. What happens if that employee leaves your organization?

*4 - Focus on succeeding at work at the expense of their families and personal lives.*

Work can become an escape from personal pressures and difficulties. That's fine. However, when it becomes a hideout instead of a place for thought and performance, it affects the individual's and the team's performance and again becomes a management issue. The workplace should not become someone's life to the exclusion of everything else.

## 5 - *Fail to use their available leave.*

There have been numerous studies on this, but if we don't take time every now and then to get away and recharge, our ability to perform at our best drops. Take the leave you have coming to you. You don't need to go any particular place. Have a "staycation" or do something else relaxing at home or in the local area. Just get away from work and its pressures and recharge yourself.

As a business owner, realize that when you reward perfect attendance, this is what you're really doing:

*1 - Paying your employees to come to work... twice.*

If your team members need to be physically present to do their jobs, why would you pay them a bonus for doing what they're supposed to be doing anyway (i.e. showing up for work to do their jobs)?

*2 - Hiding inefficiencies.*

When employees take leave or stay away when they're sick, others have to pick up their workload. Invariably having another set of eyes on a process provides opportunities to identify inefficiencies that well-intentioned team members have learned to deal with and work around.

*3 - Hiding disproportionate workloads.*

When employees are out, note how many people have to cover for just one key employee when she or he is out. If three people have to cover for one person, you're probably overloading a key person. It's time to reallocate tasks, cross-train, develop others, and really show your hard-working team members you are aware and appreciate what they do.

Dave called me early on a Monday morning. "Liz, I've got a great idea on how to motivate my employees... I'm going to give them a bonus for perfect attendance!" I had just started working with Dave's company the week before. It was a manufacturing company with roughly 175 employees. Production costs were too high. Quality was slipping and employee morale was low. Dave felt as if he were starting to drown as he tried to turn the company he had bought three years before around. So far, it was still losing money.

"Dave, let me ask you something."

"Ok, what?"

"Do your employees need to be at work now in order to do their jobs?"

"Yeah."

"Are your employees doing their jobs 100% effectively now?"

"Hell no. I told you that last week."

"I know but I needed to confirm that hadn't suddenly changed. Dave, getting your employees to show up for work isn't the issue. Getting them to show up on time and do the jobs you're already paying them to do is the issue—and that's a lack-of-management-and-employee-accountability issue. Paying a bonus won't fix that. Getting stronger management skills will."

**Here's what I suggest you do instead:** Show your employees you appreciate their work by monitoring what they do all year long. Support them by telling them to go home when they're sick and get better there. Support them by minimizing the inefficient office systems, equipment, etc. they've had to work with and work around. Support them by acknowledging that they've been carrying more than their fair share of the work and you will work with them in bringing others up to speed.

I encourage you to show your employees you appreciate their dedication. Just do it in a way that actually helps them, the other members of your team, and your organization. Base rewards on real accomplishments that actually help your team members, customers and the company move forward. Create rewards that are meaningful. Most importantly, reward your employees by respecting them enough to support them when they're sick and need time at home. These "rewards" show your employees you care for them while you also care about the business.

*"One way to make sure everyone gets to work on time would be to have 95 parking spaces for every 100 employees."*

*— Michael Iapoce, Corporate Humor Consultant*

# { 9 } Stop Thinking Your Business Can't Exist Without You

*"Talent is indispensible, although it is 'always' replaceable."*

— Felix Dennis, founder, Dennis Publishing

**WHY: IF YOU** don't build a business that allows others to participate in various aspects of it, you become the default go-to person for all decisions, all problems, and end up working more hours than anyone else. Get clear: Do you want a career or do you want to run a business?

If it's the latter, it's time to think about how you need to lead your company differently. As a business owner, a fundamental leadership responsibility of yours is to ensure the organization will continue to fulfill its mission, provide a livelihood for your employees, and products or services to your customers long after you leave. Think you'll never leave? Trust me. At some point, you will.

I had the opportunity to see one of my clients make the leap from being a manager to being a leader. I was preparing for our strategic planning session with his senior team, when Kevin, a 60-year-old serial entrepreneur, walked into the conference room and said, "Liz, I finally understand what my job is here." Now keep in mind, Kevin owns the company. He said, "My job is to create a future for this company. I need to build a strong management team to ensure this organization is still around after I'm long gone."

That's it! He "got it!" Kevin finally understood, deep in his gut, what his job as the company's leader was.

He needed to develop the management and leadership skills in his managers so they could continue to run the company when he retired. His company would no longer be dependent upon what he knew. It would be dependent upon a team of solid managers, skilled employees, and a business infrastructure that was not dependent upon any one person. If his managers developed stronger management skills, he would have time to lead, plan for the organization's future, and do the right thing for his company.

*Leadership is about what's right for the organization and the team, not what feels right for the leader.*

**Here's what I suggest you do instead:** Even though it will seem odd and might be difficult for many, this is part of a business owner's job: To ensure the continued viability and success of the organization through the sound leadership and strong management. Who better to help identify the skills, knowledge, characteristics, and insights needed of your successor than you? It is part of your job to identify, either internally or externally, the individual or individuals you believe are best suited to take over your various roles and responsibilities to manage and lead the organization into its future. Then, use your leadership skills to help them develop the skills and gain the knowledge to step into your roles one step at a time. Even though it may be personally painful, it's right for the organization. The successor(s) become the new "face" of the company. Therefore, they need to speed up as you, start to back out and prepare to move on.

So, as business owners, if developing your organization's future leaders is your responsibility, how do you do it? How do you train and develop others to take over for you when you're not trainers, teachers, or magicians? You simply need to take three major steps:

- First, believe in the urgency and necessity in leadership development yourself or no other managers or employees will.
- Second, create a clear vision and implementation plan for your organization that helps your employees see what your organization will look like in the future and

what its future managers and leaders need to be prepared to do.
- Third, establish an organization that provides development opportunities for all employees, not just a select few.

You'll need to ensure the transition to the new leader or leaders is as seamless as possible. For this to happen, help your successors not only develop their skills, but also develop relationships with the board, senior staff, and other key stakeholders with whom they will work closely in the future. You need to support your successors in earning the trust and respect of others who will be judging them and their potential to take over. Your successors will be responsible for taking over and finalizing various strategic initiatives that you started. Therefore, for their good and for the good of the organization, you'll want to set them up to succeed.

# { 10 } Stop Reacting and Start Leading With Intent

*"Great leaders are almost always great simplifiers."*

— *General Colin Powell, United States Army*

**WHY: ONE OF** the many challenges leaders face is deciding what to focus on to ensure their organizations continue to be successful. As simple as that may sound, it's much easier to say than to do. When numerous issues, project changes, and new initiatives are placed before you—a business owner—each day, it's a constant judgment call as to which ones are worthy of your time, consideration, and input—and which are better left to your managers and team members. However, effective business owners make the right call more often than not. Ineffective ones don't.

Skyler had owned his maintenance company for over 20 years. With almost 50 employees, his days were full and rather chaotic. In our first meeting, Skyler said, "Liz, I don't know what to do. I'm struggling. One of my managers said to me the other day, 'I don't know what you want!' and you know what, I don't know what I want him to do or the company to do. I'm so busy I'm burning out. I need to either get control of this thing or get rid of it."

As we talked a bit more, it became clear to both Skyler and me, he was trying to manage his business, but he wasn't leading it as a strategic business owner should. He had no vision of what he wanted for his company, its future or his own future. However, when I asked him, "Would you like to retire some day?" His response was, "Hell yeah!"

"Could you retire now and maintain your lifestyle?"

"No. I don't have anyone on my team who could take over and run it and I don't know how much I'd get for the business if I tried to sell it now."

"Well then, I guess we need to create a game plan on how you can get control of your business, clarify what you and your team need to do, and develop your business into one that will enable you to retire. But for that to happen, you need to start doing your job as a strategic business owner. If you do that, your employees will be able to do their jobs better too."

"Sounds like a great idea."

*If you, as the business owner, do your job better, your employees will be able to do their jobs better too.*

**Here's what I suggest you do instead:** If you feel overwhelmed with everything you have to do, ask yourself if you are working on things that are helping to drive your business forward or if you are you doing things that keep you busy but not necessarily moving forward towards the future you want.

If you tend to be reactive instead of intentional and strategic, honestly assess your leadership skills and consciously develop areas where you're weak. From my more than two decades of experience working with really good and not-so-good leaders, a number of skills stand out. However, to help get into a proactive, strategic mindset and role, let's focus on these seven:

**1. Think Strategically**—Think beyond the day-to-day and override the natural tendency to see the difficulties that proposed strategies might cause. Strategic thinking requires (a) business owners to focus on what's right for the organization, the employees, and the customers now and into the future and (b) a willingness to deal with intangibles, unknowns, and risk.

Strategic decisions are more often than not based upon experience and instinct, with enough research to believe the projections hold true. Strategic thinkers think about the whole organization, instead of just an individual department. Strategic thinking requires continuously pushing forward to ask, "What's next?" instead of saying, "Ahh, we've finally arrived."

2. **Identify Opportunities**—Accept that business development, business acquisitions, sales, mergers, product lines, service lines, etc. all fall in this category of opportunity identification. What is appropriate given what

your organization is, does, and should be in the future? Closely linked with strategic planning, opportunity identification often takes on a more individual approach and is done through the business owner's interactions, personal readings, tracking of world, regional, and local news events, observations during conversations over lunch, in the bank, with colleagues, etc. It is the business owner's ability to identify and fit the various puzzle pieces together that map out future business opportunities.

**3. Develop the Business Infrastructure**— Realize that any solid business needs a solid foundation. Infrastructure development requires ensuring the boring and not-so-sexy things such as policies, manuals, procedures, protocols, facilities, equipment, land, etc. are all in place to allow the organization to effectively handle current operations and, at the same time, to be well-positioned to accommodate future, more sizable work volumes. Infrastructure development is a delicate dance of not over-acquiring or over-building (and thus creating too much overhead), while at the same time, ensuring internal capacity to operate now and grow into the future.

**4. Understand Finances**—Understand what the organization's numbers are telling you in terms of where you were, where you are, and where you are going. Business owners obviously need to understand the basics of cash flow, profit and loss, and balance sheets. However, effective business owners understand how business actions and inactions can cause the direct and indirect shifts in the numbers, as well as how to enhance the overall capital strength of the organization though business revenues, acquisitions, divestures, etc. Successful business owners understand that cash is king and that big does not necessarily mean better if you can't pay your bills. Smart growth is more important than growth for growth's sake.

**5. Build Professional Networks**—Acquire or move on the gut-level understanding that strong, reliable networks of professional advisors, colleagues, associates, and friends will provide tremendous support, insight, and solid sounding-board opportunities. These networks and associates are outside the organization and will often provide straight answers and insights that internal staff don't see or are afraid to share. Professional networks provide opportunities to gain knowledge quickly and to acquire various opinions to evaluate while holding no real decision-making power or authority. They are sources of information. What's more, a true professional often provides more to the network than is ever taken away.

**6. Develop the Company Brand/Goodwill**— Protect and enhance yours and your company's reputation, for without it, your company's value diminishes. Every sale becomes harder. Every employee recruitment and hire takes longer. Every meeting with colleagues becomes a bit strained. Protecting and strengthening the company's name, reputation, and value is paramount to business ownership.

**7. Develop Others**—Knowledge transfer and developing skills in others is crucial to any business's long-term success. We've all heard, "Our employees are our strongest asset." Yet committing to developing staff is something far too many businesses fail to do. Successful businesses have for years been focusing on helping their employees and their organizations' future leaders prepare for personal and professional success. The success of the next generation of leaders will help ensure any organization's success.

*Be smart. Stop reacting. Start leading.*

These leadership and business ownership skills, insights and characteristics aren't all-inclusive, but they provide a sound basis to build upon. If the above skills were easy, every business owner would employ them. Be smart. Stop reacting. Start leading.

*"Business leaders cannot be bystanders."*

—*Howard Schultz, CEO, Starbucks*

# Conclusion

**RECENTLY, AFTER GIVING** a speech on leadership, I had lunch with several business owners. All of their businesses generate revenues of $5 million to $50 million annually. These are small, but substantial businesses with 50-200 employees each—not solo entrepreneurs.

During my presentation, I had noticed most of the audience members taking notes, nodding, or otherwise paying close attention to my comments on strategic planning, leadership styles, and organizational development. So it was again ironic, when many of the individual questions they asked of me during lunch were questions that clearly indicated they were operating as entrepreneurs not business owners. They were behaving as doers—not leaders. All but one of the business owners was intimately involved in the day-to-day operations of the business.

All but one said they often feel as if they're hamsters: *Always running to play catch-up just to keep up.* When I asked my lunch mates collectively, "So why are you in business? Why are you doing all of this work? What's it all for?" Only the one owner answered confidently, "I'm creating a business I can pass on to my children, so they can live the lifestyle they want." The others' responses were along the lines of, "We need to make money so we can retire some day."

I understand that last sentiment. However, it's not enough if you want to be an effective leader for your company.

Successful business owners realize creating a business is more than simply providing quality products or services so you make money. That's expected.

Successful business owners realize creating a business means creating a strong, viable entity that can survive without the founder or owner being intimately involved day-to-day or involved at all.

Successful business owners realize creating a business is about what the employees need so they can work with purpose and effectively serve the customers and the changing market.

Successful business owners realize creating a company is thinking of the company as something separate from themselves. They need to view their businesses as entities others will want to take ownership of and engage with. They need to create a vision, a future for the company. It's hard to do that when they're the business.

So in reality, even though they were nodding and taking notes during my speech, most of the business owners I met didn't really understand the importance of leading their businesses. They hadn't been thinking or behaving strategically. They hadn't planned for succession. They hadn't focused on building a business. They had built careers.

Until business owners create a clear vision of what the future of their businesses will be, they'll continue to play catch-up just to keep up. Instead of leading, they'll continue to be deeply involved in the day-to-day operations doing things their employees should be doing. And, from my experience, they will never stop wondering: "Why am I doing this? What's it all for?"

Remember, to successfully lead your company into the future, you need to do exactly that: lead. Realize that problems in your organization start with you.

For example:

When your team members lack basic customer service skills, it's a reflection of your leadership.

When your team members are not prepared for client meetings, it's a reflection of your leadership.

When your team members don't present a positive image of you or your business to your customers, it's a reflection of your leadership.

When your physical business structure is disorganized and ill-kept, it's a reflection of your leadership.

When your online presence is disorganized and not up-to-date, it's a reflection of your leadership.

When your team members are frustrated, unmotivated, and underperforming, it's a reflection of your leadership.

When your business has a limited repeat customer ratio, it's a reflection of your leadership.

It's time to stop doing the things that hold you and your company back from being the best it can be. It's time to start leading your business the way it needs to be led so it can become the organization you want it to be. It's time to stop working hard at business ownership. It's time to start working smartly.

# Continue Your Leadership Journey

Available at WBSLLC.com/Store

**SOMETHING NEEDS TO CHANGE AROUND HERE**
*The Five Stages to Leveraging Your Leadership*

- Are you tired of working 50, 60, 70 or more hours a week?
- Are you frustrated by what your team members don't do and can't figure out for themselves?
- Do you come in early and stay late just so you can get things done?
- Would you like to get your life back?

**IF YOU ANSWERED YES TO EVEN ONE OF THESE QUESTIONS, YOU NEED THIS BOOK!**

If you walk around complaining about your team or muttering to yourself, "Something needs to change around here," you're right. And it's probably you.

## DON'T LET 'EM TREAT YOU LIKE A GIRL® — A WOMAN'S GUIDE TO LEADERSHIP SUCCESS

With insights gathered from women and men in leadership roles, Liz shares tips to help aspiring to experienced women leaders.

**This quick-reading, insightful guide helps you identify:**

- Which leadership traits are most admired
- What your leadership brand is saying about you
- How to manage conflicts and negotiations more effectively
- What "girly" behaviors you need to STOP!

**This is a great resource for Women's Leadership programs!**

---

Liz provides content-rich, interactive, skill-building presentations to groups large and small. Liz is known for her candor and her ability to customize her topics to meet your group's specific needs.

For more information, call +1(717)597.8890 or go to www.WBSLLC.com

# About Liz Weber, CMC, CSP

In the words of one client, *"Liz Weber will help you see opportunities you never knew existed."*

Known for her candor, clear insights and straightforward approach, Liz Weber is a **sought-after management consultant, keynote speaker and seminar presenter**. She is one of fewer than 100 people in the U.S. to hold both the Certified Speaking Professional (CSP) and Certified Management Consultant (CMC) designations—the **highest earned designations in two different professions**.

As experts in strategic planning, succession planning and leadership development, Liz and her team are based near Harrisburg, Pennsylvania, and work with leaders to take their organizations:

- From no business strategy to enterprise-wide focus and clarity

- From no succession or workforce plan to enterprise-wide depth
- From a weak leadership team to a respected leadership team

Liz has supervised business activities in 129 countries and has consulted with organizations in over 20 countries. She has designed and facilitated conferences from Bangkok to Bonn and Tokyo to Tunis. Liz has taught for the Johns Hopkins University's Graduate School of Continuing Studies, as well as the Georgetown University's Senior Executive Leadership Program.

**Liz is also the author of several leadership publications including:**
- Something Needs to Change Around Here: The Five Stages to Leveraging Your Leadership
- Don't Let 'Em Treat You Like a Girl: A Woman's Guide to Leadership Success

- Stop So You Can Get The Results You Want

Liz's Manager's Corner column appears monthly in several trade publications, association newsletters, and internet resource centers for executives.

www.ingramcontent.com/pod-product-compliance
Lightning Source LLC
LaVergne TN
LVHW020930090426
835512LV00020B/3301